Birds

Ernestine Giesecke

Heinemann Library

©1999 Reed Educational & Professional Publishing
Published by Heinemann Library,
an imprint of Reed Educational & Professional Publishing

Designed by Lindaanne Donohoe
Printed in Hong Kong

03 02 01
10 9 8 7 6 5 4 3 2

Library of Congress Cataloging-in-Publication Data

Giesecke, Ernestine, 1945–
    Birds / Ernestine Giesecke.
    p.   cm. — (Outside my window)
    Includes bibliographical references (p.) and index.
    Summary: Presents a brief introduction to the physical characteristics of birds and
provides photographs and simple information to help the reader identify such birds
as sparrows, finchs, crows, ducks, and hawks.
    ISBN 1-57572-682-3 (lib. bdg.)
   1. Birds—Juvenile literature.   [1. Birds—Identification.]   I. Title.
II. Series: Giesecke, Ernestine, 1945– Outside my window.
    QL676.2.G538   1998
    598—dc21   98-6360
                                                          CIP
                                                          AC

Acknowledgments

The publisher would like to thank the following for permission to reproduce copyright photographs:

Cover: Animals, Animals/Tom Edwards

Animals, Animals/Ray Richardson, pp. 4 top, 20; Phil Martin, pp. 4 bottom, 5 top and bottom,
6 top and bottom, 8 top and bottom, 9, 15, 16, 17 top, 18, 19, 21, 22 top, back cover; Oxford
Scientific Films/Dennis Green, p. 7 top, p.11 bottom; Animals, Animals/C.W. Schwartz, pp. 7 bottom,
14; Animals, Animals/Tom Edwards, p.10; Animals, Animals/Mark Hamblin, p.11 top; Oxford Scientific
Film/Barry Walker, p.12; Oxford Scientific Film/Michael Leach, p.13 bottom; Tony Stone Images,
Inc./Gary Hayes, p.17 bottom; Tony Stone Images, Inc./Vince Streano, p. 22 bottom.

Every effort has been made to contact copyright holders of any material reproduced in this book.
Any omissions will be rectified in subsequent printings if notice is given to the publisher.

Some words are shown in bold, **like this.** You can find out what they mean by looking in the glossary.

Contents

Outside Your Window

Look! Wild animals. There are wild animals in the trees and in the air.

Some are large.
Others are small.
Some even sing.

Look closely and you will see that birds look different from one another.

Use the information in this book to learn about the birds outside your window.

What is a Bird?

A bird is an animal that has feathers. Some feathers help a bird to fly. Other feathers keep a bird warm. Birds have wings. Most birds can fly.

Birds make nests and lay eggs. After the eggs **hatch,** young birds may stay in the nest for several weeks.

wing

tail

bill

throat

chest

You can tell one kind of bird from another by looking at the color, size, and shape of their body parts.

Sparrow

This bird is a sparrow. It hops along the ground looking for food. It eats seeds and insects. The sparrow's **bill** is small but strong. It is just the right shape to crack open seeds.

You can find sparrows in the country and in the city. You may see a **flock** of sparrows fly quickly from one tree to another. You can tell a sparrow by its chirp.

MORE ABOUT SPARROWS

- Length: 5 inches (13 cm)
- Eggs: 5 to 6, white
- Nest: strings and grass

Finch

These finches eat sunflower and thistle seeds. They will come to a bird feeder near your house. Listen closely. Finches have a pretty song. A finch's song sounds like a canary's song.

Baby finches are helpless at first. Their parents must bring them food. They will fly when they are three weeks old.

Starling

You can see starlings in nearly every city. Look closely. Starlings look different at different times in the year. A starling has a dark **bill** in winter. In summer its bill will be yellow.

Adult starlings look different from young starlings. A young starling is all one color. As the starling gets older, its color changes. An adult starling is mostly dark with small light spots.

MORE ABOUT STARLINGS

- Length: 8 inches (20 cm)
- Eggs: 4 to 6, light blue
- Nest: grass and leaves lined with feathers

Crow

This big black bird is a crow. Every part of this bird is black. The crow's **bill** is thick and strong. This means the crow can eat seeds, corn, and even food scraps.

MORE ABOUT CROWS

- Length: 17 to 21 inches (43 to 53 cm)

- Eggs: 4 to 6, blue–green with dark marks

- Nest: bunch of twigs in tree

If you hear "Caw, Caw, Caw," you know a crow is near. Look up. Crows often **perch** high in the tree tops or on power lines.

Duck

Ducks spend much of their time in water.
They eat small plants that are on or near
the suface of water. All ducks have
webbed feet to help them swim.

MORE ABOUT DUCKS

- Length: 18 to 27 inches (46 to 69 cm)

- Eggs: 8 to 10, light green

- Nest: shallow bowl of grass in marsh

Not all ducks look alike. Some female ducks are dull brown. Some male ducks are brightly colored. Baby ducks can swim before they can fly.

Goose

Look for geese near ponds, lakes, and rivers. They eat many different grasses. Some geese live in the northern part of the country in summer. When winter comes, the geese **migrate.** They fly to a place where they can find food all winter long.

Look in the sky in spring or fall. You will see geese migrating. One goose flies in front. The other geese follow. The **flock** forms a V-shape in the sky.

MORE ABOUT GEESE

- Length: 22 to 26 inches (56 to 66 cm)

- Eggs: 4 to 8, white

- Nest: grass and moss on ground near water

Hawk

A hawk's wings are long and wide. A
hawk can fly far without flapping its wings.
It quietly glides in the sky looking for food.
Look for hawks in wide, open spaces.
That is where they are easiest to see.

Hawks eat small animals like rats, mice, and even small birds. A hawk uses its **claws** to catch and carry food. A hawk can even catch a bird flying in the air.

MORE ABOUT HAWKS

- Length: 18 to 25 inches (46 to 64 cm)

- Eggs: 4 to 5, pink with spots

- Nest: in tree hole or box

Feeding Birds

Put food for birds in a tree near your window. You can also put food on a porch or balcony. Watch your feeder in the early morning and late afternoon. Keep a list of the birds that come to visit.

Glossary

bill   jaws of a bird

claws   sharp nails on an animal's toes

flock   group of birds

hatch   to break out of an egg

migrate   to move from one place to another when seasons change

perch   to sit or rest

webbed   connected by skin

More Books to Read

Johnson, Jinny. *Simon & Schuster Children's Guide to Birds.* New York: Simon & Schuster Childrens, 1996.

Kuchalla, Susan. *Birds.* Mahwah, NJ: Troll Communications, 1996.

Lerner, Carol. *Backyard Birds of Summer.* New York: William Morrow & Company, 1996.

Birds in This Book

Index